# HÄGAR *the Horrible's*

## VERY NEARLY COMPLETE

# VIKING HANDBOOK

### by Dik Browne
#### with Christopher Browne

ATTICA
PUBLICATIONS

First published 1988 by Attica Publications.

Attica Limited,
DLM House,
Edinburgh Way,
Harlow,
Essex,
CM20 2HL,
England.

ISBN 1 85176 149 7

Printed in Hong Kong

This book
is for

JOAN

# VIKING WISDOM

Wisdom was always the most fragile of Viking virtues. That is because, though it was passed from generation to generation, it was, alas, passed on in a sieve.

DON'T STRAIN YOURSELF, DAD...

**N**OW WITH THIS HANDBOOK VIKING WISDOM CAN BE AVAILABLE TO ALL! ITS PAGES CONTAIN EVERYTHING YOU NEED TO KNOW, MORE OR LESS, TO MAKE IT AS A VIKING.

NO THEORIES! FACTS!

PRACTICAL HANDS-ON ADVICE FROM ONE WHO'S BEEN AROUND, KNOWS THE SCORE, WHICH END IS UP AND WHAT'S WHAT ABOUT THE BUSINESS OF BEING A VIKING.

*HAGAR THE HORRIBLE*

HIS MARK: X

# CONTENTS

The Vikings . . . . . . . . . . . . . . . . . . . . . . . . . . . 11

The Vikings at Home . . . . . . . . . . . . . . . . . . . . 23

The Vikings at Work . . . . . . . . . . . . . . . . . . . . 41

The Vikings' Real Work . . . . . . . . . . . . . . . . . 55

The 10 Most Sackable Cities in Europe . . . . . . . . . . 67

The Fruits of Victory . . . . . . . . . . . . . . . . . . . 87

Rome fell in 475 A.D.
The Dark Ages spread
    over Europe.
Civilization died out.
People got stupider
    and stupider.
Things couldn't possibly
    get worse.

And then . . . .

The Vikings
showed up
in 800 A.D.

# THE VIKINGS

# VI·KING (vī'king) *n.* 1. daring Scandinavian seafarers,

explorers, adventurers, entrepreneurs world-famous
for their aggressive nautical import business, highly
leveraged takeovers and blue eyes. **2.** bloodthirsty sea
pirates who ravaged northern Europe beginning in the
9th century.

*Hagar's note:* The first definition is much preferred;
the second is used only by malcontents, the envious, and
disgruntled owners of waterfront property.

*Historical note:* The raid on Lindisfarne in 793, which
was really a small smash-and-grab affair, is considered
the beginning of the Viking Age and the end is usually
noted as the Battle of Hastings in 1066.

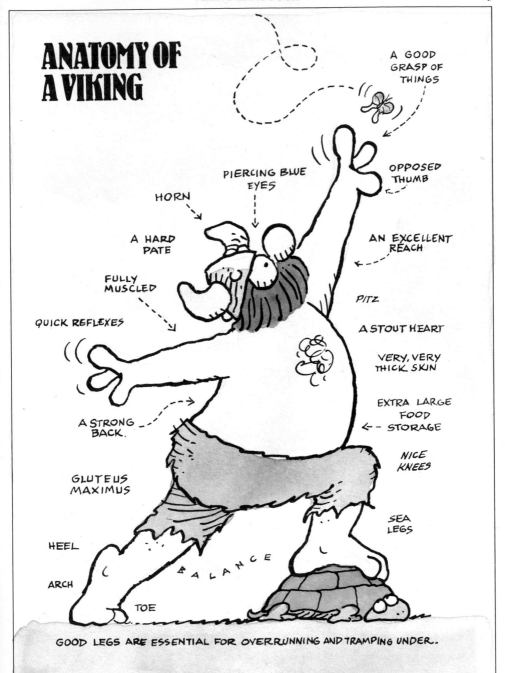

# ANATOMY OF A VIKING

A GOOD GRASP OF THINGS

PIERCING BLUE EYES

OPPOSED THUMB

HORN

A HARD PATE

AN EXCELLENT REACH

FULLY MUSCLED

PITZ

QUICK REFLEXES

A STOUT HEART

VERY, VERY THICK SKIN

EXTRA LARGE FOOD STORAGE

A STRONG BACK.

NICE KNEES

GLUTEUS MAXIMUS

SEA LEGS

HEEL

BALANCE

ARCH

TOE

GOOD LEGS ARE ESSENTIAL FOR OVERRUNNING AND TRAMPING UNDER.

# SOME FAMOUS VIKINGS

**Ragnar Hairy Breeches** (d. 860) Famed for sacking Paris, but more notable for his fireproof pants (bearskin dipped in pitch and covered with sand) which allowed him to fight the fiery dragon. His sons, Bjorn Ironsides and Ivor the Boneless, both lived up to their names.

**Harald Fairhair** (d. 930) Swore never to cut, comb or wash his hair till he conquered all Norway. Did it to impress a girl. Took 10 years.

**Eirik Bloodax** (d. 954) Harald Fairhair's nasty son. Bad-tempered even by Viking standards.

**Hagar the Horrible** (b. 940)  First Norwegian to smoke a herring (985).

**Harald Bluetooth** (d. 985)  Danish king renowned for his courage, wisdom and dental problems.

**Olaf the Stout**  Bloody Viking warrior. Later King Olaf of Norway (1015–1028). Much, much later St. Olaf. Olaf is remembered for pulling down London Bridge (1008) in a battle with the Danes, an event celebrated to this day in the classic children's rhyme: "London Bridge is falling down, falling down . . ."

**William of Normandy** (a.k.a. William the Bastard) Won the Battle of Hastings in 1066. Known thereafter as William the Conqueror.

# THE VIKING CODE

Odin, the chief god (the "All-Wise"), gave us the *Havamal,* which, added to by other Viking wise men, has become the Viking Code. Here are some excerpts, along with comments from a few lesser sages.

Look carefully around
Doorways
Before you walk in.
You never know
When an enemy might
Be there.

*HAVAMAL*

Never give a Saxon
An even break

HAGAR

Never part with your weapons
When you are in the field.
You never know
When you will need your
Weapons.

*HAVAMAL*

Happiness is being contented
With what you got
—so get enough.

HAGAR

Praise no day until evening
  No wife until buried
No sword until tested
  No maid until bedded
No ice until crossed
  No ale until drunk.

*HAVAMAL*

To the wise be sufficient.

HAGAR

Wisdom is what separates
A man from a horse—this is
Also called a saddle.

HELGA THE NATTY

The world is flat
—and crooked.

HAGAR

Write a wise saying and your
Name will live forever.

ANONYMOUS

# THE VIKING TRIBES

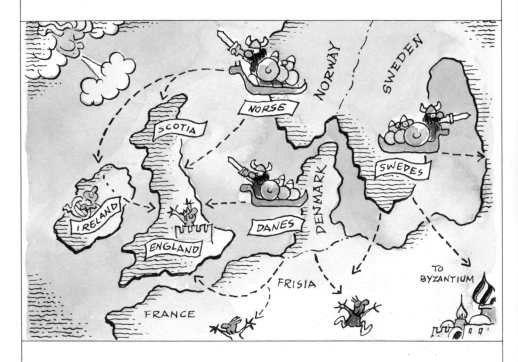

There are three Viking clans: the Norwegians, the Danes and the Swedes. They live at the very centre of the world, within easy commuting distance of major European markets.

They vary significantly in appearance (see below), and even more in their cultures and goals.

THE THREE BASIC
VIKING TYPES..

A SWEDE

A DANE

A NORWEGIAN

All Vikings like to travel, sing drinking songs and wear funny hats—but the similarities end there. Swedes are reserved, Danes are outgoing, Norwegians are just right.

Swedes are the "contrary" Vikings. Most Vikings sail west, but the Swedes like to sail east. They have a strange obsession with invading Russia.

Danes are the "partying" Vikings, much given to riotous living, open-faced sandwiches, and invading England, Germany and France.

Norwegians favour Ireland, Scotland and western England. They are the delightfully normal Vikings, devoted to lutefish and to their families. *(Hagar is Norwegian.)*

# THE VIKING WORLD

The world is flat
And that is that.

### A Poem

The Vikings need their
    Swords 'n shields
Their horn'd hats and
    Bearskins

The Vikings need their
    Swift longboats
To get away with
    Their skins

But no Viking is complete
    Without a home to run to
Without a loving wife to greet
    A daughter and a son too!

           H. the Horrible
             (age 52)

# THE VIKINGS AT HOME

# HAGAR'S TOWN

The ideal Viking port. It boasts: Ⓐ A deep fjord entry Ⓑ Ample, inexpensive docking Ⓒ A thriving business section, places of entertainment and Ⓓ Modern medical facilities. The residential area Ⓔ offers a splendid view and is only 15 minutes from the busy downtown district— 5 if you stumble.

THE TERRIBLE UNKNOWN

WHERE THE WIFFLE BERRIES GROW

MERMAID'S ROCK

Ⓐ

DR. ZOOK'S

Ⓓ

THE GEOGRAPHY LESSON

# THE VIKING FAMILY

The Viking family is *very* close-knit. The Viking Father rules the world. The Viking Mother rules the father.

Viking Daughters are often warrior maidens till age 16, when they must decide on a lifetime of fighting or marriage. Honi may, like her mother, combine the two.

Viking Sons are early to show the aggressive, good-natured cruelty so important to healthy development. Hamlet is a late bloomer.

Viking wives invented table manners.

Viking grandmothers invented relativity.

Viking women also have
had a profound effect
on their husbands'
religious life.

# VIKING RELIGION

"Take care of the gods
And the gods will
Take care of you."

There are four ways to obey this wise advice:

Know your gods. There are many deities, each with a specific sphere of influence (see page 29). Nothing is worse than a misdirected prayer.

Observe the calendar religiously (Monday—moon day, Tuesday—Tyr's day, Wednesday—Odin's day, etc.)

MOON WORSHIP

Mark all holidays with libations and burnt offerings.

Support your temple and attend the pagan ritual of your choice.

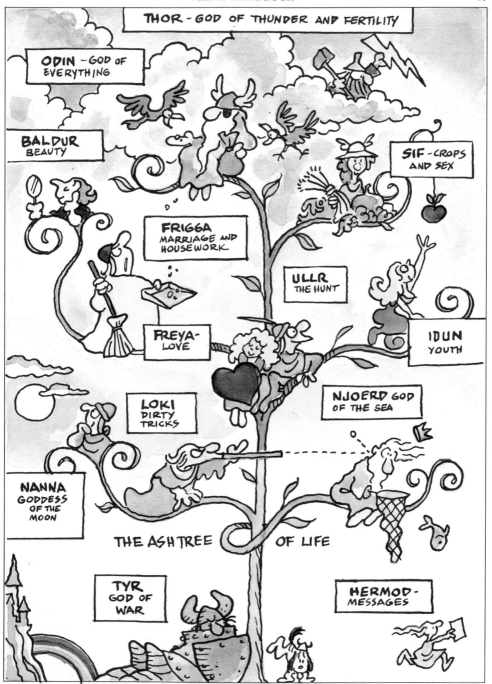

Because of the high cost of land (2p an acre) Viking houses are very compact, which makes for a home that is warm and cozy; also crowded, smelly, noisy...

# LOVE AND MARRIAGE

Viking men are really quite shy and usually meet their future wives at work.

Viking women, on the other hand, are strong, assertive and very choosy.

## Courtship

A period of not less than a full phase of the moon is devoted to haggling over the dowry while the lovers hold hands and get acquainted.

THE BRIDE

THE BRIDAL CUP

THE GROOM

## The Wedding

The ceremony is simplicity itself. The couple sips from the cup of bridal ale before witnesses and retires directly to...

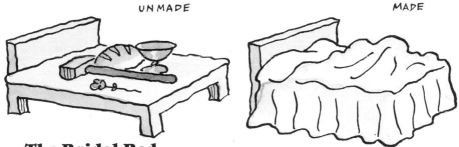

UNMADE

MADE

## The Bridal Bed

Should contain a hammer of Thor (fertility), a bread (prosperity), a cup of bridal ale (eternal love) and a thorny rose.

In a really good marriage, little things like this are easily overcome.

## Divorce

An equally simple matter. One need only repeat "I divorce you" three times in three different places to end a marriage.

"WARNING!!" THIS IS YOUR SECOND NOTICE!

# ENTERTAINING

Vikings do a lot of entertaining—especially during the
winter months, when work is slow.

> MAYBE WE
> COULD HAVE SOME
> PEOPLE IN...

First you will need a reason for a party. (And if you can't
think of one, you're not a Viking!)

You must then consider what sort of bash you want:
feast, orgy, pig-out, testimonial dinner, drinking bout,
knees-up, bacchanalia, luncheon
revel, wine and cheese tasting,
blow-out, bash.

Then you must ask yourself:
"Do I really want to have
a party?"

YES!!

You'll need something nice
to drink at your party.
Vikings are very good at
this. (They invented the six-
pack.) There's ale, mead, wine, beer. But no potable list
would be complete without that ancient holiday
beverage, gløg. Here is an old family recipe:

### Hagar's Secret Gløg Recipe

First find a foolish friend.

Then into a kettle of sweet red wine drop a
closed cheesecloth bag of cinnamon sticks,
orange peels, whole cloves...Simmer for an
hour, toss in lots of almonds and raisins, and stir
till nice and sweet.

Then...Have your foolish friend add brandy
to taste!

The actual planning of a serious Viking bash is best left
to women, who understand this sort of thing.

# OTHER SOCIAL ACTIVITIES

Many important Viking social occasions are basically family affairs, such as the justly famous Viking Funeral.

### Rites of Passage

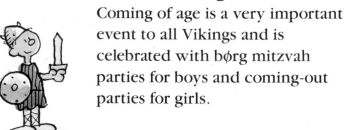

Coming of age is a very important event to all Vikings and is celebrated with børg mitzvah parties for boys and coming-out parties for girls.

There are also celebrations to mark the change of seasons and, of course, countless local festivals.

# VIKINGS AT WORK

# TRADITIONAL INDUSTRIES

## Wine Tasting

There are three things to consider in judging a wine:
① Is it free? ② How much is there? ③ Is it drinkable?

There are four additional, though less important factors:
*body, colour, aroma* and *taste* (taste is the biggie). You
will need at least one bottle to form a sound judgment,
so always have two on hand.

## Mead Making

Mead or Honeywine is *the* drink of the Vikings. Take
some nice light honey with a delicate sweet flavour, some
pretty clean water (unused, if possible), a bit of this and
a little of that. Dump it in a strong pot and stand back.
Try to keep bugs out.

## Hat Making

Classic Viking helmets are made from the metal of a fallen star and the horns of a wild, frustrated Spanish bull—which is why they are so rare. A Viking never removes his hat.

For summer wear, a perfectly good Viking helmet can be made from fruit in season.

Scoop out half a cantaloupe. Cut two holes exactly opposite each other, one inch from the edge. Peel two large bananas and insert in holes. (Feeds one.)

# BOAT BUILDING

Vikings are famous for their meticulously crafted boats.
They are blessed with great forests for wood and nice
deposits of iron for nails. But a boat doesn't build itself.

"A Viking without a boat is like
An Englishman without an umbrella."

You will need many busy hands working with true
Scandinavian efficiency. You will also need strong leadership,
dedicated attention to detail and a cost-overrun contract.

# GETTING AROUND

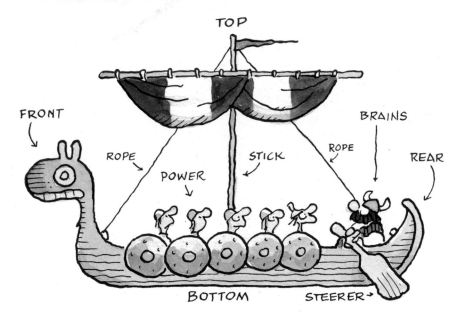

Boat building in turn led to the longboat, a really excellent way of getting around. Shallow enough to sail on a morning dew, tough enough for the most violent storm, it is powered by a sail or by oars, depending on local conditions.

The longboat is the state of the art in sailing . . .

... Unfortunately, it was poorly used for many years.

Navigation had not yet been invented, and sailors never knew where they were. Then, one magical evening, a distant relation of Hagar's—Ivor the Intemperate—awoke one night from a dream-filled sleep and beheld the outlines of wild creatures in the stars.

Navigation had been discovered!

# EXPLORATION

The development of the longboat and modern navigation opened up the wide-ranging business of colonization, which took the Vikings to strange and exciting new places.

## Iceland

So named because of its many hot springs and volcanoes, Iceland was settled by Vikings in 870. Chief products: heroes, sagas (the very best), auk eggs, smoked herring, little-bitty ponies with itty-bitty legs.

## Greenland

Developed by that intrepid real estate magnate Erik the Red, who rightly thought the name would attract more settlers.

## Vinland

Erik's son, Leif the Lucky, founded the first North American colony here. Early reports are very glowing (winters without frost, wild grapes everywhere, free wheat), but remember Leif *is* his father's son and real estate men tend to exaggerate.

There may be a future in this new world if current immigration problems can be overcome.

One of the truly great discoveries was that of Paris (860 A.D.) by Lars the Glum (later known as La-de-Lars), who spent two weeks there and is still talking about it.

Which brings us to the most important Viking business activity...

The acquisition and distribution of

Loot comes in a wide variety of forms (see page 53), but they all have several things in common. Loot is usually *imported*. It is seldom obtained without some difficulty or even risk and, most important of all, it cannot be exchanged.

So, a word to the wise:

BE SELECTIVE !

## THE WISE VIKING

## THE FOOLISH VIKING

**Good Loot**
Gold & silver
Wines & spirits
Black Forest cake

**Bad Loot**
Milk products
Itchy tweeds, bagpipes, goats
Belgian hares (in season)

## Remember these easy-to-remember rules:

Rule 1: Get!

Rule 2: Never take anything that has to be fed, watered or walked.

Rule 3: Always take two sizes larger.

Rule 4: It won't be appreciated.

# VIKING BUSINESS TERMS

**Plunder**—*v.* to obtain goods or property by great physical exertion and with considerable risk from an opponent; *n.* booty

**Booty**—*n.* the bottom line or end result of plunder

**Loot**—*v.* to plunder, pillage, sack; *n.* same as booty and plunder

**Pillage**—*v.* same as plunder; sometimes confused with pilgrimage but more violent

**Ravage**—*v.* often misunderstood; really just means to wreak havoc

**Sack**—*v.* to extract merchandise from a town after capture (see plunder)

**Rapine**—*v.* don't get any dirty ideas—it means to grab property by force

**Pilferage**—*n.* cruddy little stealing

VIKINGS DON'T PILFER!

# THE VIKINGS' REAL WORK

# EMBARKING & DISEMBARKING

GET GOLD AND JEWELS APLENTY —AND IF THEY HAVE IT IN MY SIZE, A NICE DRESS THAT I COULD USE FOR THE HOLIDAYS... NO SHORT SLEEVES! ...I HATE SHORT SLEEVES...MAYBE A DOLMAN ...IN SILK..BUT NOT GREEN.... AND A NICE LEG OF LAMB FOR MY MOTHER...

THE SAD FAREWELL

Departures are both exciting and sad. After weeks of feverish activity, the boat is fully loaded. A few last embraces . . . and finally the ritual reading of the "list of wishes."

## The Happy Hour
Waiting for the sun to set over the yardarm.

Disembarking is much trickier than embarking. There is seldom a handy dock, and often arrows, rocks and insults are being hurled at you. Be sure to follow these easy-to-follow instructions: Ⓐ Be very certain you want to do this Ⓑ Mount the gunwale (the side of the boat that sticks out above the deck) Ⓒ Bellowing a fearful oath, jump! Ⓓ Make sure the water is no deeper than three feet.

# TACTICS

Vikings have only two basic tactics. One is a massed charge called the Boar's Snout. (Note the little ears?)

For defense they rely on the Shield Wall—which is good, but only as strong as its weakest link.

# THE GRAND MELEE

Most Viking battles soon degenerate into melees in which everybody hits everybody else.

Surprise is always a nice element. For this you can't beat the Berserkers, the fiercest of the Vikings, who go into battle stark naked with such frenzy that they bite their shields.

# BASIC COMBAT

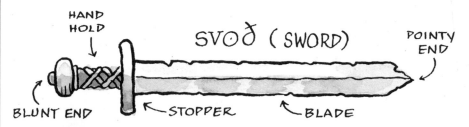

HAND HOLD

SVOð (SWORD)

POINTY END

BLUNT END — STOPPER ← BLADE

WRONG!!

A Viking's most prized possession is his sword. Old swords are the most prized of all, because only good swords get to be old swords.

Caution: Never point a weapon, loaded.

Here are the four basic movements of swordplay:

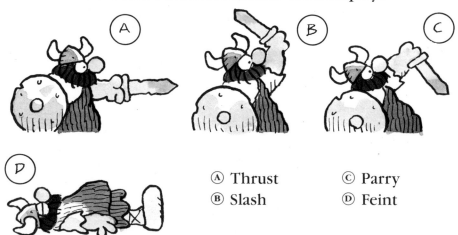

Ⓐ Thrust     Ⓒ Parry
Ⓑ Slash      Ⓓ Feint

# THE BROADAX

"Sword for show but broadax for dough."
—Old Norse saying

This is *the* Viking weapon.

Axes come in many sizes, but they are all irons and hit in exactly the same manner. Plant feet comfortably apart. Sweep blade back (do not bend left arm) and execute full body turn. The return swing should start with the torso and end with a full follow-through. In battle, need we add, keep your head down.

Grip is very important. Here is the approved overlapping-intertwining grip.

# STRATEGIC WEAPONS

Catapults are necessary for larger targets. This model is the MX Missile Launcher (named for the year of its invention).

## Loading

A relatively simple operation:

Ⓐ Remove cocklegear

Ⓑ Release lanyard tension

Ⓒ Tip device to vertical position, and

Ⓓ Load missile

## Firing

Gently tip device to original position. Aim and fire.

A trained crew can fire the catapult several times a day.

AIMER

RELEASER

MOVING MEN

# THE CASTLE ASSAULT

(5 approved approaches)

**Assault Towers**
Effective but expensive (building is sky-high). Also flammable.

**Catapults**
Highly effective but destructive to property.

**Battering Ram**
Quite direct, but renders user susceptible to hot oil, slings and arrows.

# VIKING ANNUAL REPORT

Castle sacking is fun, but it's not where the money is . . .

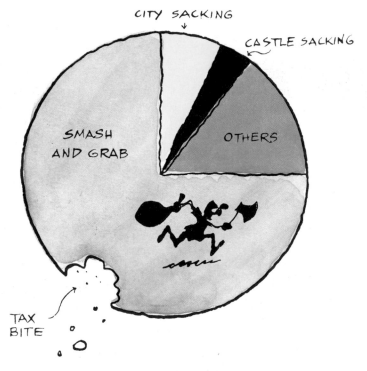

More than 75% of Viking income comes from smash-and-grab raids against monasteries, waterfront resorts and isolated cow barns. A promising new sector accounts for 10% of the total (up from 8% last year), because of which we have included a special section on this fast-growing business . . . **City Sacking**

# THE 10 MOST SACKABLE CITIES IN EUROPE

★ ★ ★ ★    Excellent
★ ★ ★       Good
★ ★          Fair
★            Ugh

# TRAVEL TIPS

But first, a few general tips about European travel.

You will be going to countries with many different customs and manners—do not be too judgmental!

• You will find that some people eat with *forks*. This does not necessarily indicate either weak or dirty fingers—it is merely a local custom.

• Learn a few foreign words or phrases: "Where is the toilet?" "Give me your money." Foreigners will be flattered and it will speed up your visit.

• Do not bring money into a foreign country—but do bring money out!

• Relax and enjoy yourself—you'll get a lot more out of your trip.

Disclaimer: Some of these cities may have come under new management since this book was written. We cannot be responsible for changes in service or cuisine.

# LONDON ★ ★ ★

Any sacking of Europe should begin with London—it's the city with everything, and it's so conveniently close.

The English have a reputation for being standoffish—a complete exaggeration, as are stories about their weather.

## Dining Out

If you like English weather, you'll love English cooking. Try Bubble and Squeak, Spotted Dog, Toad-in-the-hole, Blood Pudding. Every bit as tasty as they sound.

## Best Bet

London tailoring is world-famous. Don't deny yourself this pleasure!

## The Natives

The English call everybody by their last name. Do not take it personally.

# DUBLIN ★ ★

Ireland is so new a market that the Vikings have been forced to build cities to loot. Dublin is due to open about 1050 A.D.

## Best Bet

There are many excellent Best Bets (harps, lace curtains, first novels), but the true Irish art is chemistry. Try the "erse usquebagh" (Irish whiskey) and other products.

MAKING IRISH CREME LIQUOR

## The Natives

The Irish are a warm, witty, and highly imaginative people—do not ask them for directions.

# EDINBURGH ★ ★

Easily reached by either the high road or the low road.

THE MATURE MALE SCOT IS EASILY RECOGNIZED BY HIS BEAUTIFUL PLUMAGE AND LOVELY COLOURING

HILL    TOWN    CASTLE

MALE        FEMALE

## The Natives

Very clannish, terse, tartaned. Formerly known as Picts (now Scots), they no longer paint their bodies blue but favour busy textiles (plaids) and haggis (the stomach of a dead sheep, with all the trimmings) and, when excited, play bagpipes.

## Best Bet

A delightful local wine which the natives call whiskey and everybody else calls Scotch.

SCOTTISH INDUSTRIES — TARTAN MAKING

# PARIS ★ ★ ★ ½

Paris is well worth sacking any time of the year,
but Paris in the spring . . . tra la, tra la . . . is truly an
experience. A must for any Viking.

## Dining Out

The French are famous for their cooking. They can make a princely meal out of *nothing*! Among French delicacies, do try snails, amputated limbs of amphibians, pressed duck, abused goose liver, and fungus.

## Best Bet

High fashion is the attraction here, but don't overlook the excellent wines and nice cheeses.

## Language

The French are proud of their language. Its lovely sounds are full of delicate nuances. Do try a few French sentences— it is sure to amuse the natives.

# COLOGNE ★ ★ ½

Cologne and the Rhineland offer something for everyone. Famous for beer and eau-de, the city is also noted as a pretzel centre. Octoberfest, which celebrates the arrival of spring, is usually held in July.

Getting there is half the fun—an easy sail down the Rhine, taking in the river's many lovely sights.

## Best Bet

All Vikings love a good sword and the very best come from Cologne, but they are expensive. Vikings buy their swords here, raid Cologne to pay for them, then use the proceeds to buy more swords. This is known as a balance of trade.

## The Natives

Germans are very formal. If you meet one, it is correct to lift your hat and shake hands a lot.

## Worst Bet

Two things to avoid because they travel badly are Limburger cheese in summertime and cuckoo clocks at any time.

# ZURICH ★ ★ ★

Zurich is where the gold is, which is why this modest city in the foothills of the Alps rates three stars. The gold flows from all over Europe into banks without number.

THE LORD ALPS THEM THAT ALPS THEMSELVES

FOOTHILLS

BANK
BANK
BANQUE
BANCO
BANK
BANK

LAKE OF ZURICH

Getting the gold out of Zurich is truly a monumental challenge because it is guarded night and day by the famous Gnomes. Zurich is also known for zither plucking, high-alto yodeling, and earplugs.

GNOME DE PLUME
↓

## Best Bet

Look for the world-famous swiss cheese, but beware: make sure it is real Swiss.

AUTHENTIC   IMITATION

## Dining Out

The national sport of Switzerland is Fondue Dipping. Do try it. The rules are simple: if you drop the bread into the bubbly goo you must stick your head in the fondue pot.

## The Natives

The Swiss are the neatest people in Europe. Do not litter while sacking or you'll be in trouble.

# ROME ★ ★ ★ ★

This is the one city you have to sack before you can be taken seriously as a genuine threat to civilization. Rome is somewhat picked over by now, but it still has much to offer the dedicated plunderer. Take your time. After all, "Rome wasn't bilked in a day."

## Dining Out

While in Rome try everything, except a diet! Linguine, fettuccine, cannelloni...but *not* "uno stuzzicadenti" (you'll get a toothpick).

## Language

There's no language problem in Rome. The Italians have perfected a beautiful system of hand gestures that any intelligent person can understand—with a little study.

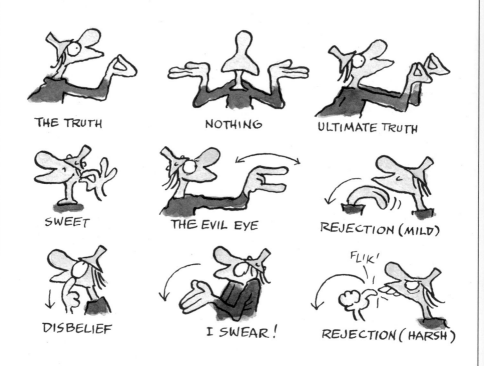

However, it's always nice to know a little Italian, as long as you don't get caught.

# VENICE ★ ★

## How To Get There
Sail up the Adriatic looking carefully for land. When you don't see any, that's Venice.

CAMPANILE

SAN MARCO

DUCAL PALACE

BRIDGE OF SIGHS

PIGEON

Undoubtedly the most accessible city of the top ten. Sacking and looting can be done without ever leaving your longboat.

## Best Time To Visit
High tide.

## Tipping
Never tip a gondolier.

## Warning
Pedestrians always have the right of way.

# MADRID ★ ★ ½

This is a place to try for a change of pace after those long northern winters. In addition to sunshine, it offers hair oil, guitar picks, bottle corks, matador capes, sangría, castanets and bull horns.

## Timing is all-important.
The ideal time to sack Madrid is during siesta (1:00 P.M.–4:00 P.M.). But try not to disturb the natives—they are deadly if their sleep is interrupted.

Remember, Madrid is also a place for fun. Try Spanish dancing. Get a suntan. Eat an orange.

Spaniards are strangely fascinated by horns. Once again, do not take it personally.

**Travel Advisory**

"Under New Management" is a common sign in Spain due to conflicts between the Moors and Spaniards. Check the latest information before invading.

# NOVGOROD ★

DOWNTOWN NOVGOROD

THE GREATER NOVGOROD VODKA WORKS

TWO GUYS FROM NOVOSIBIRSK

SUBURBAN NOVGOROD

THE CHERRY ORCHARD

THE LOWER DEPTHS

Novgorod is ideally located for visits by both Swedish and Finnish Vikings. Today it is a leading city of Russia, with extensive iceworks and a booming business in wolf traps —plans are being made for an excellent road out of town.

## Dining Out

Most places serve musk-oxtail soup, carrion in aspic and, of course, borscht. This last is an acquired taste.

THIS CREAM IS SOUR!

## Best Bet

However, people do not come to Novgorod to eat! They are drawn by that magical restorative elixir "Vodka," so precious that its export is strictly controlled.

Also check out the twin cities of Minsk and Pinsk.

**MINSK** "Who is sick of Minsk is sick of life" is as true today as when it was first written in 518 on a suicide note.

Minsk is ofen called "The Gateway to Pinsk."

**PINSK** is merely a lesser Minsk.

A PINSK NEGLIGEE

**A FEW HELPFUL PHRASES**

| | |
|---|---|
| Мне хочется!! | BOOZE !!!! |
| Здравствуйте. | HANDS UP! |
| Нам пора итти. | LET'S SPLIT! |
| Я вас люблю. | HI, BABY! |
| Передайте привет вашим тёте и дяде. | SAME TO YOU WISE GUY! |

And then there is
# BYZANTIUM

The golden horn. The dream of every Viking. The jeweled carrot—just out of reach. The horses that pull the rubbish wagons wear shoes of gold.

But it's a wise Viking who knows when to quit, to pack up his profits and go home before the winter winds blow.

# THE FRUITS OF VICTORY

After the loot has been distributed to the grateful family and deserving crew, a first-rate Viking will find he has a lot left over. This can be a problem in a small house with few closets.

You can invest it or play it safe and put it into land.

Now will the north wind rage; ice will bar the unknown sea, longboats will stay in port, people all over Europe will sleep in peace . . . the Viking is at rest.

For a Viking there is a time and a season for all things . . .

A time for war...     A time for peace.

A time for bringing in...     A time for taking out.

A time to sing...     A time not to sing.

A time to feast . . .

A time to fast.

A time to lead . . .

A time to be led.

A time for raising up . . .

A time for putting down.

And a time to talk

A time to look back

A time to look forward

## A time to plant

## A time to plan

## A time to. . . .

*Editors note:* The age of the Vikings is said to have ended with the battle of Hastings and the conquest of England in 1066 . . .

... but don't you believe it.

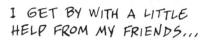

## Thank You To:

Robert "Chance" Browne
L. M. Schneier
Ralston "Bud" Jones
Bruce Blackistone
William Jessop
Dick Hodgins III

And very special thanks to
our editor, Michael Cader
And, of course,
      Peter the Workman